Mind over Manners

Poems, Discussion and Activities About Responsible Behavior

by Greta Barclay Lipson, Ed.D.

illustrated by Dan Grossmann

Teaching & Learning Company
1204 Buchanan St., P.O. Box 10
Carthage, IL 62321-0010

This book belongs to

_____

Cover photos by Images and More Photography

Copyright © 1999, Teaching & Learning Company

ISBN No. 1-57310-186-9

Printing No. 987654

Teaching & Learning Company
1204 Buchanan St., P.O. Box 10
Carthage, IL 62321-0010

Table of Contents

iii

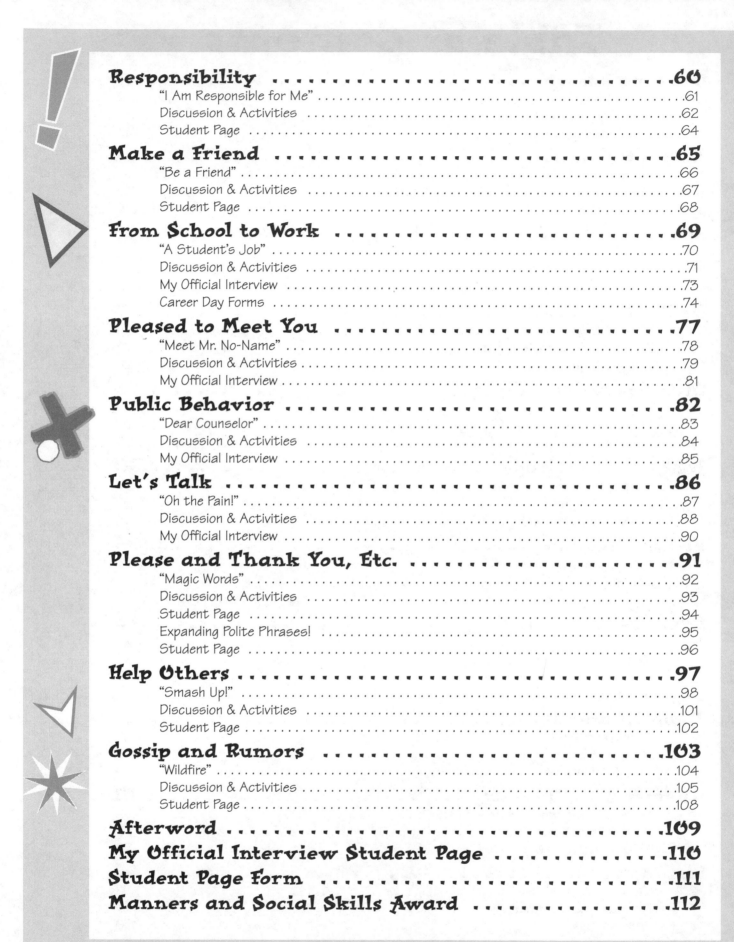

Dear Teacher or Parent,

Sometimes you are called upon to explain the importance of something so common-sensical, that it becomes daunting. This is the case with good manners. Because manners are such an essential part of daily life and just because we are all agreed that they matter—it is nevertheless beastly hard to explain why manners are important.

Because the home is the critical place where manners are demonstrated and taught, there will be some exercises in this book which will involve adults at home. In the format of this book, an occasional (one question) interview page will be included as a take-home exercise for the student. We hope this sharing strategy will give the manners lessons substance and that the lessons will be grounded in the real world of home and school.

Good manners define the values of society. Everyone is obliged to act properly no matter what their age, social level or economic circumstances might be. Manners furnish us with a code of behavior so that we have expectations and an understanding of how we should act toward one another. Good manners help make us civil, courteous and respectful of one another.

On a daily basis, manners grease the wheels of civility at home, in our neighborhoods, at work and play. We have a fair notion of what to expect from one another and what our personal responsibility must be. Such a social code helps to make our lives somewhat predictable, kinder and more trouble-free when we know how to act and what to expect from others.

This understanding of appropriate and responsible social behavior does not come automatically. It must be modeled by significant adults. Negative behavior must be the cue for "a little talk"—since "laissez faire" (non-interference) does not work! Conversely—courteous behavior must be reinforced and acknowledged with positive and supportive words. It must be encouraged on all levels of endeavor: at home, at school, between friends, neighbors and most especially, where it all begins—in the home from family to kids.

One of our objectives is to invite comments and ideas from home which may be expressed on students' interview pages. These lessons on manners then become a joint undertaking in which school and home give each other valuable support. This is an opportunity to implement a cooperative effort to make behavioral issues clear.

Display the introductory poster for each chapter in your classroom to highlight each concept.

Sincerely,

Greta

Greta Barclay Lipson, Ed.D.

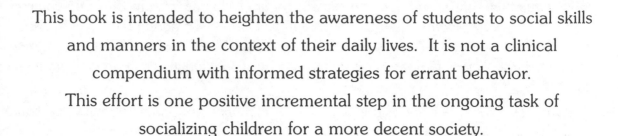

How to Use This Book

This book is intended to heighten the awareness of students to social skills and manners in the context of their daily lives. It is not a clinical compendium with informed strategies for errant behavior.
This effort is one positive incremental step in the ongoing task of socializing children for a more decent society.

Why don't kids act properly in social situations? According to scholarly literature,* children do not act properly in social situations for three reasons:

1. They may not know the desired behavior.

2. Their emotional responses may inhibit their behavior.

3. They may know the behavior but lack the practice.

Teacher will . . .

- Read the opening selection
- Ask for reactions:
  what is the lesson about?
  what is the students' point of view?
  what advice would the students give?
- Initiate activities and encourage innovation
- Act as moderator and arbiter

Students will . . .

- Listen to the opening selection
- Discuss and write about the topic
- "Act out" any scenes of choice
- Initiate creative ideas
- Respond to the Student Page

*Cox, R.D., and W.B. Gunn, *Interpersonal skills in the schools: Assessment & curriculum development.* In D.P. Rathjen and J.P. Foreyt (Eds.) *Social Competence: Intervention for children and adults.* New York: Pergamon Press, 1980.

Opening Lesson

- Ask the following big questions of the entire class.
- Discuss the answers.
- List answers to these questions on the chalkboard.

What Are Manners?

Use your dictionary to find a definition of *manners*.

My dictionary says, in part, "a way or style of doing something. A socially correct way of acting; etiquette, the prevailing customs, social conduct, and norms of the specific society, or group. The way in which a thing is done or happens. A way of acting, bearing or behavior."

What Does Social Mean?

Another dictionary task: Find the definition of *social*.

Living together in communities, neighborhoods, schools, relating to society, living together in organized groups.

What Are Social Skills?

Use your dictionary again to find a definition of the word *skills*.

My dictionary says, in part, "To be an expert in doing something. Doing something well; developed through training and experience."

Caveat

America is a mix of many cultures. Remember, there may be people in your school or neighborhood who observe different social conventions than we. Be aware of this—and respect and allow for those differences.

An Analogy

Analogies often help to illustrate a concept concretely. Think about manners in terms of rules of the road as a perfect example. Consider the four-way stop street for motorists. Everyone knows the rule and observes it. Each driver arrives at the intersection at a slightly different time.

The rule is that drivers each take their turn and proceed with caution. This arrangement goes on all day long, all week, all month, year after year. The beauty of it is that it is a procedure that is understood by everyone on the road, including pedestrians and bikers. It is not necessary to have a police officer present to enforce the law.

An Analogy

- Imagine, in your mind's *eye*, what would happen if no one observed the four-way stop street law! Draw a picture of that intersection without the law. What is happening? Who is getting mad and where are the cars? The pedestrians are trying to cross the road. School kids are anxious to get home for lunch. Even Cheeter, the dog is upset! He knows he's got to wait for the traffic to clear.

- Now! How can you apply the described situation (about the reasons for traffic laws) and apply it to manners and social skills? (Answer: Our day-to-day lives would be unsafe and unpredictable. We wouldn't know what to expect from others. In short, our existence would be disorderly and dangerous!) To *generalize* means "to draw conclusions from a broad situation and apply them to specifics."

Act Out

Host Speaks to the Class:

"Good evening, ladies and gentlemen. I am your host, Maddy (or Manny) Manners with another show that will demonstrate to you the reasons for traffic rules. Try to apply this situation to social rules of behavior as well."

"We are on Pingree Street where there seems to be quite a commotion among the motorists and the pedestrians at a four-way intersection! There are no stop signs here and nobody seems to know what to do. I have a few drivers here who would like to explain their side of the story and the reasons for their anger. We will try to keep the situation calm. We hope they don't start shouting at one another!"

Characters Introduce Themselves:

Mr. Gabby (a big-mouthed driver): He thinks he owns the road and isn't shy at all. He wants the right of way and doesn't care about anyone else.

Ms. Nicely: A quiet and courteous driver. She has been sitting at the intersection for a long time, but others keep going through and don't give her a chance.

Mr. Meek: A frustrated driver who is afraid his new car will get smashed if he takes a chance and starts through the intersection.

Cheeter, the dog: He knows enough to stand and wait until traffic clears. He is fed up with all the humans! He's tired and wants to get home because he's hungry.

Name _____

My Official Interview
Student Page

You may ask an adult at home or any interested grown-up of your choice.

Question

What are three important manners that you think kids need to practice?

_____

_____

_____

_____

_____

_____

_____

_____

_____

_____

_____

_____

The person I interviewed was a _____

(parent, relative, neighbor, family friend, teacher)

Signature _____

10

Respect Yourself

You are a piece of work!

You are **worthy**, **important**, and in your way you will make a contribution to the **greater good** of the human community. First, you must care enough about yourself to be **careful** and **sensible**. Hold your mind and body in high regard. You have been making choices since the time you were little and those choices become more and more important to your future as you grow. We are told that in order to give love, we must first *love ourselves* and *understand* the miracle of being alive. That **self-love radiates from you**—out to others in the form of **self-esteem**. The wonder of it all is that **YOU are one of a kind** in a world population of 5.77 billion*. And can you imagine that there is no one else in the world who is absolutely, completely like you? **Accept** yourself, **protect** yourself, **make healthy choices** and think of yourself as a **wonderful** cosmic *gift*.

*The World Almanac, 1997.

Body Dumpster

Hey, dude,
You wanna be cool?
I'm in the shadows
Over here where we can sneak around.
Would you like a great high?

Just once is all—you sniff, snort, smoke, drink or shoot
If you don't like it—nothing lost
Don't be a wimp
It'll get your heart really thumping clean out of your chest.

Or how about a seizure?
Or a blissful coma?
Or some other big-time fun
Like a body bag?

Nothin' to be scared of
Don't listen to the stupid do-gooders!
After a while you won't care about a thing . . .
Not family
Not friends
Not your brains or guts or eyeballs
And certainly not school!

Hey, dude,
You wanna be cool?
You're your own boss!
Right?

G.B. Lipson

Respect Yourself

- There is a very important message here, which is: "always protect your mind, your body and your self-respect." Never be duped into doing something which you know is bad, dangerous, stupid, pointless or which you will regret deeply. Bad actions have bad consequences—so use your head and think ahead and beyond the moment. When in the 1980s First Lady Nancy Reagan said, "Just say no!" it sounded too easy. In truth it is a strong position that you can take though it may take practice.

- Explain the meaning of **consequences**. This is in bold print because many grown-ups believe that young people do not realize that if a person does something really foolish or dangerous, that person will have to pay for it in one way or another! Sometimes more than one person must suffer the consequences (such as your family). What does the word *consequences* mean? ("Something that logically follows from an action that may have a widespread effect.")

- What things might kids do that would have "consequences"? Think about the metaphor of throwing a stone into a pond and the effect of circular ripples that radiate outwards—on and on and on.

Act Out

Ask for volunteers to play a scene in which a very persuasive person is trying to talk some kids into trying some illegal substances. "The bad stuff" is the actors' choice. How would the students refuse? Find out what could happen to someone who used alcohol or illegal drugs. (A person could be fined, suspended from school, be jailed, addicted to drugs, seriously blemish school records, affect mental and physical health. Or—you could die from one foolish act.)

Respect Yourself

Act Out

Ms. Judith Martin, a respected authority on etiquette is also known as Ms. Manners. She was quoted as saying that some folks have the misconception that manners are so constraining that it amounts to "martyrdom" in the effort to please others and make them feel comfortable. These "other people" (it is assumed) may then feel free to do as they wish. Her answer to this assessment is a resounding "Absolutely not!" Ms. Manners says there are times when you will have to "upset" people and assert yourself.*

Ms. Manners Says:

What does Ms. Manners' statement mean to you as an individual? (You can have good manners and still not be a wimp.)

At the Teacher's Discretion

Collect items in newspapers, magazines and on the internet which are relevant to kids regarding firearms, drugs, tobacco and alcohol. (It was reported in *The New York Times* that on Friday, September 26, 1997, an 18-year-old freshman at Massachusetts Institute of Technology attended a party off-campus in a fraternity house where he was pledging. At that party he drank five times the legal limit of alcohol for driving and no one stopped him. He lost consciousness, his heart stopped and he never woke up. It was hard to believe that such a bright boy, a scholastic achiever and a fine athlete was capable of such a senseless, tragic act. Dr. Henry Wechsler of the Harvard School of Public Health, and other professionals, cite binge drinking on American campuses as a grave problem.)

*_Unte Reader_ (a bi-monthly magazine) Sept.-Oct. 1997 issue, "Talking Stick," page 37, Lens Publishing Co., Inc., Minneapolis, MN 55403.

Name _____

Respect Yourself

When you are invited to do something stupid, and you are smart enough to be afraid, what are some things you can say or do to get out of a bad situation?

_____

_____

_____

_____

_____

_____

_____

_____

_____

_____

_____

_____

_____

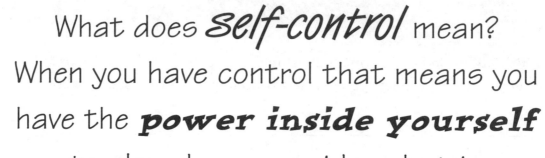

What does *self-control* mean?
When you have control that means you
have the **power inside yourself**
to slow down, consider what is
happening and then act appropriately.
It means that something may happen
that makes you angry, burned up mad
and ready to lash out at somebody or
something—but you don't!
Instead you **manage yourself**
well enough so that you do not do
something hurtful to yourself or others.
You do not act out like a wild animal.
You *cool out*,
settle down,
think things through
and then *act*.

Settle Down

He sputtered and he choked;
The steam blew out his ears.
He shouted and he croaked
As he blinked away his tears!

It was so awfully sad
To see him suffer so.
Whatever made him mad
We fear we'll never know.

We'd like him to explain,
But he can't even talk.
We ask him who's to blame?
He only kicks and squawks.

Did someone misbehave?
Whoever is to blame?
Unless he learns control
He'll always be the same.

G.B. Lipson

Self-Control

- Describe a time when you got boiling mad at someone! What made it happen? Were you right or wrong? Did that make any difference?

- What did you finally do to calm down? Were you able to talk things out or have a discussion with the person who was responsible?

- Some people have a strategy that works for them: they sit down and write a long letter that expresses their anger. They write everything they want to say which helps them get it out of their system. And then . . . they tear up the letter. How would that help? Can you describe a "cool down" strategy which might work?

- Remember–there are some things that are said in anger that can never, ever be taken back–even though you say you are sorry. What may those spoken words be? ("I hate you"; "I'll never speak to you again"; "I never liked you";"You're not my friend anymore.")

- If you were the kind of person who blurted out everything that came into your head, how would people feel toward you? Why?

Act Out

Think of a situation where tempers flare. Act out a scenario where Emily went poking around into Danny's precious baseball cards and he gets steamed. They both get into a terrible argument and are snarling at each other. It looks as if it will never be settled. Now act out the same situation where either Emily or Danny try to cool down and find a solution that is satisfactory to both of them.

Name _____

Tell about a time when you were proud of yourself because you controlled your emotions or your actions and didn't lose your temper.

I was proud when . . .

_____

_____

_____

_____

_____

_____

_____

_____

_____

_____

_____

_____

Be Positive

As much as we can, it is good to
be positive in our daily lives.
Look on the *bright side*, be **optimistic**,
think the best of people,
try to **be upbeat**,
BE PROUD of yourself
and *let the sun shine in!*
According to ancient Greek mythology,
humans, unlike animals, were created to
stand upright with **dignity** and lift
their eyes toward the horizon to fulfill a
unique and shining destiny!
This is a word picture that has an
inspiring message for all of us and
supports our **hopes** and
aspirations.

20

Be an Upbeat Kid

Be an upbeat kid
Let your heart take flight!
Suffuse your mood
    With cheer and light.

Open the sky
Harness the sun
Float with the clouds
    And run, run, run.

Bounce in the waves
Welcome the night
Dazzle with stars
    Distant and bright.

Sail the world
Reach for the moon
Toss leaves from the trees
    And sing a sweet tune.

Slide on the ice
Capture the snow
Dance in the rain
    Grab a rainbow!

Hold your good fortune
Near to your heart
Be glad you're alive
    Your joy to impart!

G.B. Lipson

Be Positive

- There is something in the topic poem "Be an Upbeat Kid" that suggests a picture or a mural full of energy and high spirits! In a class art project, incorporate some of the visual images found in the poem on butcher paper with materials of your choice. Give the picture a title that captures the upbeat mood.

- Look up two words.

    Optimist: A person who expects the best possible outcome or one who expects the most hopeful aspects of a situation to develop.

    Pessimist: A person who takes the gloomiest view of a situation and thinks there is more bad in the world than good!

    Which kind of person are you? Head your paper "I believe I am (an optimist or a pessimist)." Can you tell why you think that is true?

- There are many sayings about people who view the world in a happy or in a miserable way. A popular expression is "An optimist sees a glass of water as being half full. A pessimist sees a glass of water as being half empty." If a person says, "Every cloud has a silver lining!" is that person an optimist or a pessimist? Explain. Find axioms that you think express these two opposing attitudes.

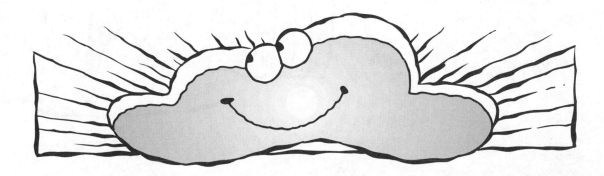

Be Positive

- Nobody can be happy and upbeat all the time. All of us, kids and adults alike, have ups and downs through the week and that is natural. But there are ways of helping ourselves and making things better. An important way to feel relief is to have someone you can talk to and help to get things out of your system. We call this "trouble talk." Who are the kinds of people that kids (or grown-ups) talk to in order to get the bad feelings out (a good friend, a relative, grandparents, a minister or rabbi, a parent, a teacher, a coach)? These people are important, *not because they tell you what to do, but because they listen to you.*

- David Burns, the author of the book, *Feeling Good: A New Mood Therapy*, thinks that people have faulty ways of thinking, and that they may expect too much of themselves. What are some things you don't have to expect of yourself? As a class, can you suggest some things you don't have to be or things you don't have to do?

1. I don't have to be first, or best.

2. I should not exaggerate my faults.

3. I do not have to be the smartest.

4. I should not say bad things about myself.

5. I do not have to (student choice) . . .

Thinking in this positive way are there more things you can add to this list that will be helpful in your feelings toward yourself?

Name _____

Be Positive

I can be a positive person because I am grateful for many things in my life! Some of the things in my rainbow are . . .

_____

_____

_____

_____

_____

_____

_____

_____

_____

_____

_____

_____

_____

Give Everyone a Chance

School is a place where each of us, in our own way, has an **opportunity to learn**. This is true on the baseball field, or in math class, or in shop class, or in English, or in band or chorus or computer class. Everyone should be given a favorable time to **try** his or her **ability** in activities at work or play in school and out. This is the time to find out about **skills** and **strengths**, about **ways to improve** and about the hidden **talents in all of us!** School is not a business for profit—it is a **place of discovery** and **learning** for young people where there is *room to grow!*

Opportunity

A person is a creature
Who's covered by a hide
And wonder of all wonders
Is the brain that is inside!

You may be tall and strapping
You may be fat or thin
You can't tell from the outside
What wonders lie within!

There's a powerhouse of smart stuff
Inside of every brain
Respect that great potential
That could bring a person fame.

There is no way of telling
What someone's mind can make
They could be quite the genius
And that would take the cake!

So give everyone a chance, my dear
Include them on your team
Though they may not show much talent
They may find the next vaccine!

G.B. Lipson

Give Everyone a Chance

- What is the poem trying to say to the reader? (People have potential for achievement and one can never be sure how far our abilities can take us. Never discount the capability of a person's mind, hands and heart.)

- We have all had the experience of being surprised by someone who turned out to be rather smart in astonishing ways. Even if you haven't had that experience, think it through and develop a story that starts:

  Everybody thought he or she was stupid until one day . . .

- For real surprises about exceptional people who had to fight for a chance, find some biographical information in the library or on the computer that deals with famous people who have overcome great obstacles. These obstacles may have been handicaps, public resistance, a lack of acceptance or countless other reasons.

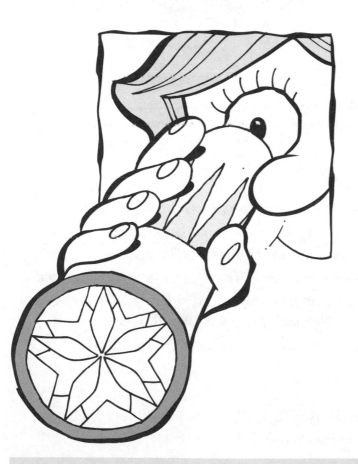

- I like to think that human beings are like kaleidoscopes! A kaleidoscope is a tube-shaped optical instrument that is rotated to produce many kinds of symmetrical designs by means of mirrors and bits of colored glass. When held up to the eye and turned in the light, the fascinating bits and pieces inside change patterns with every turn. Human beings have the same capacity to produce a wonderful variety of personalities and achievements. Find a kaleidoscope you can look into!

Give Everyone a Chance

- Use a compass to produce a symmetrical design to simulate the beautiful pattern of a kaleidoscope. Color in with paint, crayon or markers. Your design will be a metaphor for your personal qualities and your complexity! (A metaphor is the use of dissimilar things to reveal a strong similarity between them: "Juliet is the sun.")

Act Out

Imagine a role play where Alexander Graham Bell has invented the telephone, and he goes to an investor, Mr. Big Bucks, for financial support to get his invention on the market! Mr. Big Bucks questions him closely and comes to the conclusion that a phone is a ridiculous toy! Do your best, Alexander, to convince this fellow otherwise!

For the Teacher

Professor Howard Gardner, of the Harvard Graduate School of Education, is a pioneer of the theory of multiple or different kinds of intelligences. He deplores the notion that intelligence can be measured as with a "metal dipstick." There are many human intelligences, and there is not a single entity called smartness. He opposes the unitary theory of intelligence. He posits that biological, psychological and anthropological evidence supports his view.*

*The New York Times, Section A, p. 21, Nov. 1, 1997, "Lofty Ideas That May Be Losing Altitude": Intelligence Testing, compiled by Janny Scott.

Name _____

Give Everyone a Chance
Student Page

In answering this question, be brave and honest!

I would like a chance to . . .

_____

_____

_____

_____

_____

_____

_____

_____

_____

_____

_____

_____

_____

_____

What's an Attitude?

Perhaps you have heard somebody say, "She's got an **attitude**!" You know right away that it is not a compliment because it describes someone whose manner or moods are unpleasant. Often people with an attitude make others feel bad because of the things they say or the way they act to those around them.

To **keep safe**, people prefer to avoid anyone with an attitude. Another way to define attitude may simply be that you have a

good *(positive)* outlook

or a bad (negative) outlook. Language can be tricky so *try to say what you mean.*

Puhleeze!

He looks down his nose whenever we talk
He doesn't say a thing that's nice
It's not what he says, it's the way that he says it!
Does he think he is better than everyone else?
Does he wonder why people stay away from him?
He never says "Hello"
It's like he's too good for everybody
He thinks the rules don't apply to him!
He refused to give his name when he was stopped in the hall
He thinks he doesn't have to do what is expected
He wouldn't sit in his assigned seat
He yawned loudly all the way through the class!
He just up and leaves and never says "good-bye"
He gives our school a bad reputation
He has no interest in any of our team efforts
He gives the substitute teacher a bad time
He's just plain rude!
        and on
                and on
                        and on
                                and on.

                G.B. Lipson

The character in this poem may be "he" or "she" depending upon one's point of view!

What's an Attitude?

- In the poem on the previous page, are there some kinds of behavior that should be included in a description of people with an attitude? What would you add to the list?

Act Out

Ask for volunteers for dramatizations: Who wants to be the teacher? Who is willing to be a student with an attitude? Have two dramatizations to demonstrate a kid with an obnoxious attitude.

1. As he or she is just entering the room.

2. As he or she is already in the room.

Make a general plan about the two situations and what is going to take place. How would you, as the teacher, deal with students who think they are better than everyone else and that the rules do not apply to them?

Thumb through magazines and newspapers to find pictures of people who, by their appearance, seem to have an unpleasant or superior facial expression. Though you cannot really tell by a picture, it can be interesting to see what impresses you as being arrogant (high and mighty). Cut these pictures out and write a fictional thumbnail sketch of these characters. What are their names? How do they earn a living? What are their interests?

In an acrostic form, the letters of the subject are written down (vertically) to form the word of choice. Next to each letter, the descriptive statement is written horizontally to express the subject in innovative ways. Our example is the word *attitude*. Look this over and compose an acrostic of your own.

I'm Bad!

Anytime I see them I sneer.

Then I say something insulting.

Too bad if they don't like it!

Is it embarrassing for them?

That's exactly what I want!

Until they know I'm top dog

Do they bend my way?

Everyone is careful around me.

G.B. Lipson

Name _____

What's an Attitude?

Think about a person on television, in the movies, in sports, in a music group, in a book or in history with a bad attitude. Describe this character.

_____

_____

_____

_____

_____

_____

_____

_____

_____

_____

_____

_____

_____

_____

_____

_____

34

Praise Pays

When someone makes a nasty remark and makes you feel foolish, or dumb, or unattractive, or diminished—it is a bad experience! Unfortunately everyone has had that experience.

We all need the *assurance* that **we are significant**, that *we are worthy* and that *we matter* to others who care about us as human beings.

All of us need to know that **we count** for something because, in this world, *every single unique human being is important.*

Everyone of us can **make a contribution** in this world, no matter how great or small that share may be. We all need to be told by others that we **have special qualities** and we need to *hear good things* about ourselves from others. It costs nothing to **give praise** and it is a treasure to the one who receives it.

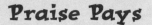

No Put-Downs, Please!

A true story from Ms. Generous, sixth grade teacher

Ms. Generous walked into the teachers' lounge looking dejected. "What's the matter?" asked one of her colleagues. "You look like you've lost your dog."

"It's not quite that bad." She tried her best to smile. "But I just don't know what to do with my sixth grade class." She sighed and sat down unloading her books on the table crowded with coffee cups, student papers, pencils and the usual teacher stuff. As always, there were a few sympathetic listeners who wanted to know what was going on.

"Well, it's like this. It seems that every time my kids talk to one another they are insulting. They hurt one another's feelings. They say rotten, miserable things to one another and usually somebody gets hurt and then puffed up and is ready to start pushing and shoving! They are forever putting one another down. It's like they are trying to outdo one another."

"Hey, I get the picture," the gym teacher piped up. "And I have the solution." Everybody was listening now. "They've got to make a special point of practicing saying good things about one another and not allowing anyone to express something rotten. It's got to be like a campaign or sensitivity training. You know what I mean?"

"I think I get it," Ms. Generous shook her head. "We'll talk about nasty remarks and how hurtful they can be. And then we'll discuss how good it makes you feel when people make positive remarks. If they were just civilized with one another it would help. I know they all hate the 'put-downs.' We'll make banners that say: 'Down with Put-Downs!' 'Praise Pays' or whatever else the kids dream up to make them more aware of how they are wasting one another."

She got up to leave and seemed to perk up with new energy, "I'll try it. I've got nothing to lose!"

Praise Pays

- **Stop Put-Downs!** Organize some campaign strategies for your classroom which you think will begin a whole new attitude toward ending insulting remarks between classmates.

Act Out

Set up a scene in the teachers' lounge when Ms. Generous comes in and tells her story to a few teachers present. What advice would others give her? There are a few different points of view!

If you are prepared to make banners for this campaign, what would they say that would announce your meaning to anyone who reads them? Praise Pays; No Put-Downs Here; If You Can't Say Something Nice, Don't Say It; A Compliment Is a Boost.

It is wonderful for everyone if you make a kind remark that will make someone feel really good for the rest of the day! Make a list of five (or more) of your classmates. Write a compliment next to each name. Hand these in to the teacher who will process these and read them (through the week) to elevate the morale of *every* student. Use an organized strategy to spread the praise around. Do whatever it takes to make sure no one is excluded.

Praise Pays

This exercise needs student courage and teacher supervision. Select a pair of children to sit in front of the room. Each student must be prepared to say something good to his or her partner. This activity should be brief and include only a few participants at a time. The teacher should model this "encounter" first and make sure that no one is excluded. Some examples are: "You're a good sport"; "I like the way you draw"; "You have a great smile"; "You know how to share"; "You help people a lot"; "Your red shirt is my favorite."

Assemble a class book entitled, *People Boosters* with complimentary pages for each student. Outside contributions (from other teachers, relatives and friends) are welcome. **Caution:** However difficult this may be–the teacher must make certain that every student has equal representation in the book.

Mount these complimentary pages on designed construction paper. Display them for everyone to see, in or outside of the room. When they have been adequately displayed, assemble in the *People Boosters* book. Mobiles will also work artistically.

The greatest praise of all can be from the teacher! Have your students bring in postcards which are self-addressed. Write a compliment a week to just one student until each person has received that special teacher mail for everyone at home to read!

What is the best compliment you can remember receiving? Who gave you the compliment? If you are brave enough, you can tell the class. If you prefer, you may write it down and share it with the teacher.

Name _____

Praise Pays

Student Page

If you could receive the most wonderful compliment in the world, what would that compliment be?

_____

_____

_____

_____

_____

_____

_____

_____

_____

_____

_____

_____

Say, "Hello"

When you enter a room for the first time at home, school or business or you pass people on your way, you **announce yourself pleasantly** with a greeting. You may use "**Howdy** or *Hi* or **Good morning**, or *How're you doing.*" It is your choice of salutation as long as you address folks in a *courteous manner.* A pleasant greeting also says something about you. It tells people that you are an **open and warm person** and that the goodwill of other folks is important to you.

If you don't do this, it is regarded as unfriendly or self-absorbed or uncaring. People do not like to feel invisible or unworthy of your recognition, and a *"hello"* **takes very little effort.**

Hello There

Hello, hello, hello, hello!
It starts with H
And ends with O.
Hello, hello, hello!

It's even good
If you say "Yo"
'Cause we all know
It means "hello."
Hello, hello, hello!

Say howdy doo
or heidy ho.
It starts with H
And ends with O.
We like to hear you say "Hello"!
Hello, hello, hello!

Somedays you might feel just so-so
And not so very friendly-o.
But still you've got to say "Hello"!
Hello, hello, hello!

There's one more thing
Along with "Hi!"
That's when you leave
Please say, "Good-bye."

Hello, hello, hello!

G.B. Lipson

Say, "Hello"

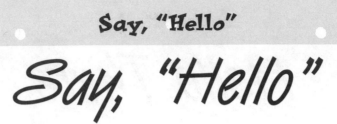

Hel - lo, hel - lo, hel - lo, hel - lo. It starts with H and

ends with O. Hel - lo, hel - lo, hel - lo! It's e - ven good if

you say Yo, 'cause we all know it means hel - lo. Hel - lo, hel - lo, hel -

lo. Say how - dy doo or hei - dy ho. It starts with H and
days you might feel just so - so and not so ver - y

ends with O. We like to hear you say hel - lo! Hel - lo, hel - lo, hel -
friend - ly - o. But still you've got to say hel - lo! Hel - lo, hel - lo, hel -

1 lo! Some

2 lo! There's one more thing a - long with H! That's

when you leave please say good - bye. Hel - lo, hel - lo, hel - lo!

Music by H. Goldman and The Campbell Group.

42

Say, "Hello"

- The question I heard most often when I was talking to adults about manners was: Why don't kids say "hello"? Do you know the answer to that question?

- What greetings do people use in other languages? It may not translate exactly as "hello." Talk to your parents, family and friends. Is your greeting included in the phonetic spellings below? The following list was compiled by Ms. Geraldine Barclay's bilingual class at Fitzgerald High School in Warren, Michigan. The spelling was a problem, but the students did the best they could according to the sound.

Language	Greeting
Bulgarian:	zdrasti
Russian:	zdrastvuite
Arabic:	mar haba
German:	guten tag
Greek:	yasoo
Assyrian:	schlama
Polish:	czesc
Spanish:	ola
Italian:	ciao
Urdu:	salaam
Hmong:	nuaw le ka
Vietnamese:	loi dung de chao
Comanche:	haa
Croatian:	hola
Ukranian:	dobriden
Zulu:	sawubona
French:	bonjour

Say, "Hello"

- Talking about foreign languages reminds us of the town of Sdrawkcab (Backwards). Their greetings are much the same as ours. It just takes a little more time to figure out what they are saying! Write down these salutations from a Sdrawkcab student; then decode them.

Olleh, woh era uoy?	(Hello, how are you?)
Woh od uoy od?	(How do you do?)
Olleh, ti si ecin ot teem uoy!	(Hello, it is nice to meet you!)
Od ton tegrof eyb-doog!	(Do not forget good-bye!)
Semitemos I yas ih.	(Sometimes I say hi.)
Semitemos I yas os gnol.	(Sometimes I say so long.)
Eyb, eyb!	(Bye, bye!)

Name _____

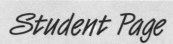
Bring one or more old greeting cards to school. Redesign your own card with cut-outs from the commercial card. Cut and paste the decorations onto a folded piece of bright construction paper. Your opening message may be–"Just wanted to say 'Hello.' " Continue with a friendly message.

_____

_____

_____

_____

_____

_____

_____

_____

_____

_____

_____

_____

Table Manners

Eating meals together as a group or a family can be an *enjoyable experience.*

When people are relaxed and want to talk about the events of their day—sitting around the table at mealtime is a **wonderful opportunity for sharing**.

Even if there are just two of you it can be a **special time** to **nourish the body and soul**.

Be sensitive about the topics you discuss over meals.

It is not the time for disagreeable subjects.

Be **kind** to your digestion and everyone who shares a meal with you. *Good manners* always matter, whether at home, in a restaurant or as a guest.

So **ask** for things *nicely*, **take your time**, chew with your mouth closed and help make your meal a *pleasant and smooth experience.*

Don't Bolt Your Food

Don't bolt* your food;
You're not a dog!
Don't oink your food;
You're not a hog!

Please be civilized
And don't be boorish.
Eat your food nicely
Your body to nourish.

Good table manners
(We needn't mention)
Will help your stomach
And aid digestion.

Use your napkin
For whatever drops.
Wipe up those messes;
Don't be a slop!

Courteous kids
Are always allowed,
So sit up straight
And make us proud!

G.B. Lipson

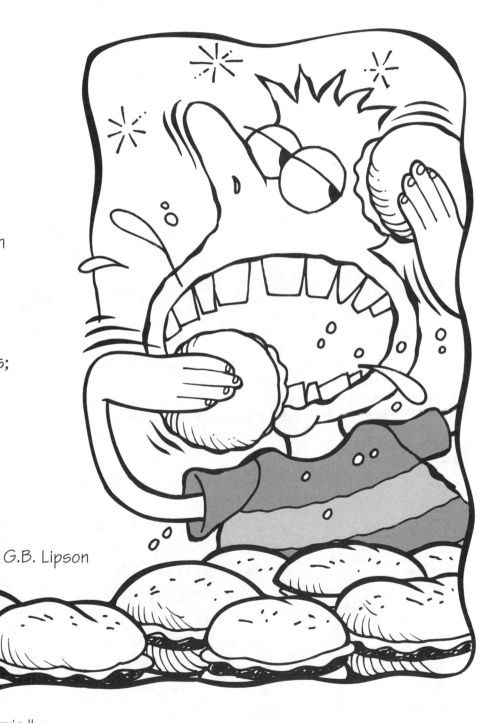

*bolt: to gulp—to eat food hurriedly

Table Manners

- Charlie Chaplin was a famous comedian in olden times. He made a classic movie in 1936 called *Modern Times* in which he worked on the assembly line in an automobile factory. An inventor came along who designed a feeding machine–the idea being that it would save money and time since the worker would not have to leave his place on the assembly line while he ate. The machine went berserk and had Charlie in its grip tossing him about as if he were a rag doll. The machine was feeding him feverishly and wiping his face with a napkin until it blew up in one colossal wheeze! Keeping this in mind–your assignment is to plan a weird, funny invention that will help people at mealtime. Go get 'em!

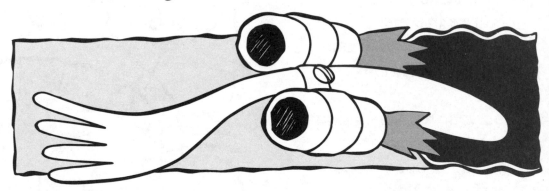

- Help create a list of Dos and Don'ts table manners:

Dos

Wash your hands before a
    meal.
Wait until everyone is seated.
Use your napkin.
Pass food to the right.
Make sure everyone has a
    share.
Finish the food on your plate.
Help clear the table.

Don'ts

Eat with your mouth full or
    open.
Tell offensive stories.
Comb your hair, blow your
    nose or cough.
Pick at someone else's food.
Slurp your soup.
Put your fork or spoon into
    the serving dish.
Dig into your mouth with a
    toothpick.

Table Manners

- Sometimes we sit down at a meal in someone's house and the flatware is set rather formally. You don't have to panic! Just start with the outside forks or spoons and work your way in toward your plate. Forks go to the left and the napkin next to that. The knife goes to the right next to the plate. A soup spoon and/or teaspoon is to the right. Generally we are not in formal situations but when you are unsure, it is wise to watch others. You may even ask and nothing bad will happen.

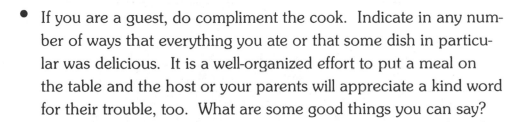

- If you are a guest, do compliment the cook. Indicate in any number of ways that everything you ate or that some dish in particular was delicious. It is a well-organized effort to put a meal on the table and the host or your parents will appreciate a kind word for their trouble, too. What are some good things you can say?

- At home or away, as a considerate person, volunteer to help clear the table, or scrape the plates or stack the dishes, or put things away! Even if your offer to clean is refused, it shows a willingness to share the task of neatening up.

Act Out

Host (to the class):

"Good morning, ladies and gentlemen. I am your host, Maddy (or Manny) Manners with another show on The Worst and the Best of Table Manners. We have as our guests today, Sloppy Sheila who will demonstrate how not to act at the table. Sitting at the same table with Sheila will be Proper Paul who will demonstrate how to act properly at a meal. Please hold your comments until after the presentation."

(Other characters of choice may be included in the skit.)

Props:

Use paper and plastic props for flatware, dishes, napkins, salt and pepper shakers, bowls, drinking glasses.

Name _____

Table Manners

You may ask an adult at home or any interested grown-up of your choice.

Question

Describe the most special meal you ever had, when you had to use fine manners.

_____

_____

_____

_____

_____

_____

_____

_____

_____

_____

_____

_____

The person I interviewed was a _____

(parent, relative, neighbor, family friend, teacher)

Signature _____

Answer That Phone!

The telephone is an essential part of our lives.

It keeps us **in touch** in our personal and business affairs, and we can hardly imagine what it would be like without it. As in all other communications between people, there are **important rules** of **telephone etiquette** to observe which make the process work efficiently. A telephone *voice* should be **crisp** and **strong**, messages should be taken carefully and transmitted **accurately**. In business today there is a standard script when the operator answers and then asks, *"How can I help you?"*

Though you needn't answer that way at home, it is good to remember the **HELPFUL STYLE!**

Answer That Phone and Sound Alive!

I called this weirdy kid at home;
My voice was clear and strong.
He answered like a guy half-dead,
So I thought I had dialed wrong!

"Are you okay?" I asked straight out.
"Do you have the strength to talk?"
He cannot move his lips, I thought.
"Can you move or can you walk?"

His voice was thin and very weak.
"Did I dial the morgue?" I cried.
He mumbled something in the phone.
He sounded like he'd died.

"I have a serious message," I said,
"And I'm sorry to trouble you so.
But your folks have won the lottery
And I wanted to let them know."

I heard him choke at the end of the line,
But nary a word said he.
"Please take the message," I begged of him,
But he ignored my plea.

They didn't get the message.
I am very sad to say . . .
So the money went to someone else
Who answered the phone the right way!

G.B. Lipson

Answer That Phone!

- How do you answer the phone? How do you take a message? What problems do you have, if any, with the phone?

- If you must run all over the house to find a pencil and a piece of paper when you take a message, how can you remedy this?

- Here is a great hint for everyone: If you cannot remember an important telephone number, look at the key pad letters and make a word out of the numbers. (My favorite is "key stag" which stands for 539-7824.) If you can't find a word, try for a pronounceable combination as in KLY-NIVY. Try it!

Act Out

Organize several partnerships to demonstrate **appropriate** ways and **inappropriate** ways to answer the phone, to take messages or to announce a call to someone in the house. Take the time to plan your scenario and make your skit effective. Perhaps you have had a weird phone experience. Don't lose your sense of humor. (I once made a call to a family, and the message I heard on the answering machine was left by a barking dog–no humans, only the dog!)

Contact your local telephone company to ask for any available booklets which discuss proper and safe telephone manners. How much information should you give over the phone? What information is off-limits? Why?

Answer That Phone!

List the rules for taking messages accurately. (Even some adults need the same instruction as children in this regard.)

1. What time did the call come in?

2. What is the name of the caller? Ask for a spelling of the name and repeat the spelling when you are finished.

3. What is the caller's number, including area code?

4. What is the message?

Invent a new kind of telephone with super features! Draw a picture of it and describe its new and revolutionary use. Give it a name.

If you are in someone else's house and you are asked to answer the phone, what should you say? ("Hello, Cuthbert residence.") What clue does this give the caller? Should you answer the phone in someone else's house? Why?

Review the rules for dialing the 911 emergency number in your community. Remember it is reserved for life-and-death situations, which is why the computers trace your call instantly! Some people do not understand this, and they call 911 for problems which do not require immediate assistance. This poor judgment diverts the service away from people who are in genuine trouble.

If you had the responsibility of making some rules about the use of public telephones, what would those rules be? If the phones are public, which means that anyone can use them, what is the reason for having regulations? (Some people settle down to talking as if they were at home. A public phone is just that. Other patrons expect to have the use of the phone without waiting half an hour to make a quick call.)

Name _____

Answer That Phone!

My Official Interview

You may ask an adult at home for the following information.

Question

What are some telephone rules observed at home which include courtesy and safety?

_____

_____

_____

_____

_____

_____

_____

_____

_____

_____

_____

The person I interviewed was a _____

(parent, relative, sitter)

Signature _____

Listen

Someone once said that *"listening is an art."* When you **LISTEN**, you *make an effort* to hear something. You **pay attention**, you **TUNE IN** and you make the speaker feel as if *what is spoken has value* and is **meaningful**. You receive, you process in your brain and you **respond**. You engage the eyes of the speaker and do not drift off in other directions. Even your body language and facial *expression reveal* that you *care*. Sometimes there may be an interruption in the flow of **conversation** and the speaker may ask, "Now where was I?" If you can reconstruct the conversation, and say, "You were telling me about your Grandpa's wild chickens. Remember?"—that is the greatest compliment of all to the speaker.

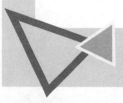

Someone Who Listens

The beauty part is
Talking to you!
Because you listen
And you listen with
Brain and heart.

No interruptions
No wandering interest
You face my face
And there we are
Eye to eye.

You listen—You pay attention
You make me feel that what I say has meaning and value.

You wait to ask a question
And then you listen
For an answer!

I don't feel that everything I say
Is monumental.
That would be the fool's way.

It's only that you listen carefully
And make me feel
Good!
And I thank you for that
Courtesy.

G.B. Lipson

Listen

- The listening in the poem is of a personal nature involving talking and listening about feelings. There is a kind of attention that we expect from people we talk to. What do you think those signals are that tell us that we are being listened to? (Eye contact, a shaking of the head, certain words that are sympathetic . . .) What are the clues that tell us that someone is not listening? (Interrupting, doing something else at the same time, asking a question and not waiting for the answer, no response in words or action.)

- I was recently interviewed by a newspaper reporter. She had a tape recorder and she also took notes. We talked for a couple of hours, but there were some details that were inaccurate in her printed story. Arrange a short interview with a partner. Ask one important question. Concentrate on the facts. Recount the details of that interview in a presentation to the class. Be accurate!

- If you had an especially bad day and you wanted very much to talk to someone, what would you expect from that person? Whom would you talk to–a friend, a parent, a relative . . . ?

- There are words that have certain intense poetic quality all by themselves. For that reason there are many books and poems that have the word *listen* or *hearing* in the titles. Make up book titles or general titles that contain one of those words. Make them as interesting as you can. (Listen to the Night; Hear Distant Songs; Listen to Anger; No Ears to Hear; Nobody Listened to Buddy!)

- There is another kind of listening which we do which also requires attention–but is not personal. What are these other kinds of signals that we hear and understand immediately? (We listen to police and fire sirens, church bells, warnings, clock alarms . . .) Your brain is like a grid that sorts out the sounds that are important to you. Draw a funny cartoon (nonscientific) of a "selective brain" which lets in signals that mean something to you.

- A play was performed on television based upon a novel by G.D. Gearino entitled, *What the Deaf Man Heard*. It is about a man who pretended to be deaf for 20 years from the age of 10. He and his mother were traveling on a bus at the time. His mother left the bus, briefly, but was hurt and never returned. The last thing she had said was, "Not one word out of you, not one!" This meant that for 10 years, in his make-believe deafness, he overheard things that would never have been spoken in his presence, had people known he could hear! What are your feelings about this story?

Name _____

Listen

Write about an embarrassing experience you have had because you were not listening!

_____

_____

_____

_____

_____

_____

_____

_____

_____

_____

_____

_____

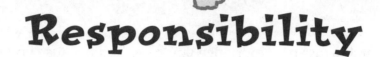

Responsibility

RESPONSIBILITY is the hardest quality to develop. It means *being accountable* for what we do.

It means we are on our way to **growing up**

and having to stand up and say, "I can do that job,

I will **do what is expected** of me **without excuses**,

I will **do my share** and you can **DEPEND UPON ME**

for whatever I promise to do.

If I make mistakes, I will *not blame others*, or if I do not

fulfill my task, or if I am foolish,

I'll try to **do better** next time."

The best part is that the ability to do many things

increases as we *grow* and *learn*.

And so does the capacity to use **good sense**.

I Am Responsible for Me

Sure, I want to be grown up
So, let's understand what that means:

No! I'm not a baby anymore,
That means a lot of things.

Like if I do something dumb—
I can't blame anyone else.
If I fail at a task,
It's my failure.
If I make a mistake,
It belongs to me.
If I am ditzy, it's my behavior.

Then there's the good stuff—
I am dependable.
I've got both feet on the ground.
I am there when you need a helper.
I keep promises.
I share the load with family and friends.
I can be trusted.
I am honest.
I think about consequences.
I am what I seem to be.

Sometimes it's hard to be responsible—
I have to face some hard times!
I have to face some uncomfortable moments!

But I'm not a baby anymore!
Trust me!

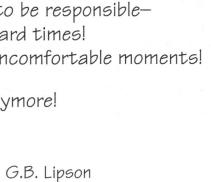

G.B. Lipson

Responsibility

- First, in your own words, try to explain what you think the word *responsibility* means. Give examples of responsible behavior. (Doing chores around the house, taking care of your dog or cat, helping a brother or sister, getting all your clothes and books ready the night before a school day, keeping your room clean, doing your homework when you should without being nagged . . .)

- The poem says, "It's hard to be responsible," and it suggests that it can be hard and it can be uncomfortable. Think about it and write a paragraph about what it is that can sometimes make responsibility "hard and uncomfortable." (Not doing what someone expected you to do, admitting that you neglected a chore, taking the blame for a foolish thing you did, having to say you are sorry! . . .)

- A synonym is a word that has almost the same meaning as another word as in: happy, satisfied; night, dark; funny, humorous; walk, stroll. Look up the definition of the word *responsible* in the dictionary. Write the definition. Now find some synonyms which help explain the word (reliable, honest, dependable, trustworthy, faithful). The dictionary will give you synonyms, but a larger source is a thesaurus. Look for one in your classroom or library.

Responsibility

- As you get older you begin to take on more responsibility. The reason is that as you mature you understand more, you are physically and mentally capable of doing more things and your judgment develops. Take a piece of paper and fold it lengthwise down the middle. In the left column print *Then*; in the right column print *Now*. Think of the things you did when you were little and what you can do now because you are older and more capable.

- There is so much to look forward to as you grow older and more responsible! What purchase is very special in your dreams? Draw and cut out a large pair of eyeglasses with fun frames! Paste these on a folded construction paper booklet and entitle it, *Looking Forward to . . .* Inside draw a picture of, or write a description of, that special item you would like in the future. Include details: Cost? Care? What kind of responsibility do you think is involved in your choice?

Name ______________________________

Responsibility

Student Page

What are your responsibilities outside of school, and how do you feel about them? Do the responsibilities make you feel more grown up?

Make a Friend

We all need friends.

They are there for us for **fun**, for **support**, in **good times** and bad. *Friends give* us another point of view, **advice**, a *shoulder to cry on,* a different look at ourselves, **belly laughs**, shared experiences, *respect,* **ReGaRd,** honesty, **admiration** and food for thought. The *most special thing* about friends is that (unlike relatives) you pick your own! Usually our friends have a **VARIeTY OF PeRSONALiTieS** and each one fills a different need.

Like a gem, each good friend is a **unique** cut—*precious,* **COLORFUL** and *worth a lot.*

Be a Friend

To make a friend
Be a friend!
And how do you do that?

You help
You give
You listen
You are there when you are needed.

You share ideas, hopes, dreams
You laugh together
You respect and admire each other
You share your friend with others.

You do all of this not just when it's convenient!
Not selfishly.
You work at it
You give comfort
You are not peevish.
You are kind and thoughtful.

So when you give so much—
Be sensible about your choice!
Choose a friend for all the right reasons
Be honest with yourself.

Because when you choose a friend—
You open your heart and offer a portion of yourself.

G.B. Lipson

Make a Friend

- Attention! Attention! There are some very important statements in the introductory description of friends at the top of the opening page! "The most special thing about friends is that you pick your own." Make certain that your choices reflect well on you. You are known by the character of your friends, and they should be the kind of people who make you proud. The next item of importance is that your friends must respect you, have a high regard for you and admire you. If you have a buddy who makes unpleasant remarks to you or about you, puts you down or humiliates you in any way–it is time to leave that relationship and say good-bye! Sometimes people will say, "I was just kidding!" or "I meant it as a joke," but don't believe it. Nobody needs hurtful treatment from someone who pretends to be a friend. You must protect yourself from such individuals! Has this ever happened to you?

- What are the characteristics of friends? Think carefully about this question. With class participation, make a web chart on butcher paper using colored markers. This can be an astonishing graphic collection of personal qualities which you expect in your companions. On the other side of the coin, you may ask: "What characteristics do you stay away from?"

- Buddies, friends, companions and mates are often the topic of songs. Find the words to songs, old and new, in which the theme is friendship. Write out lyrics to be read or recited in class. If someone can perform on an instrument or bring in a music tape or a CD, that would be an interesting event!

- With help from your librarian, search for a book that deals with the topic of friendship. Find a story that you think is really great! Deliver a book talk that will capture the interest of others and persuade them to read the book, too. Don't tell the whole story, but do stop in a place that will make your classmates want to trot right over to the library.

Make a Friend

Student Page

Describe a wonderful thing a friend once did for you.

_____

_____

_____

_____

_____

_____

_____

_____

_____

_____

_____

_____

_____

_____

_____

From School to Work

Amazing as it may seem—all young people in school have a serious job! Your job is to **do the best you can** in reading, writing, arithmetic and **thinking** in all subject areas so that you are ready to be an adult with **skills** and the ability to *pursue a career.* You are even **LEARNING IMPORTANT LESSONS** while you are having a great time at play. The *wonderful mystery*, which is locked away during your early schooling, is that most of us have no idea what we will be doing to earn a living when we are grown up. What you are *learning* now may seem like kid stuff, but it is serious **preparation** for things that you will be doing in *your future* as an adult.

On pages 74-76 are the forms and plans from Harding Elementary School in Ferndale, Michigan, where Career Day has been observed, with invited guests, since 1992. Adapt these documents to your school.

A Student's Job

Just in case you thought you didn't have a job—here is your huge job description! You may add to it as you wish.

I Am Practicing:

To be a grown-up

To be a good person

To respect myself and others

To be a good family member

To be a fully developed person

To be a skilled person

To be loving and kind

To be honest and ethical

To be courageous

To be happy

To be well-liked

To keep learning

To fulfill my potential

To cherish a free society

To be thankful!

I am practicing to serve and care for . . .

family, community, country, humankind, nature and all living creatures.

G.B. Lipson

70

From School to Work

- What do you think social skills and manners have to do with getting a job? (The answer is that in any job you must be courteous, cooperative and be able to work in harmony with other people, though you may not even like some of them!) The workplace is the final testing ground of your ability to get along with many different kinds of people from different backgrounds.

- Sometimes, when you are a young student, you have the idea that when you grow up you will have the freedom to do whatever you like. But the truth of being an adult is that **everybody** has a boss! If you think about the adults you know, you may come to realize that we must all answer to someone higher up!

  1. Who is your teacher's boss? (The Principal)

  2. Who is the principal's boss? (The Superintendent of Schools)

  3. Who is the superintendent's boss? (The Board of Education)

Even the President of the United States of America has to answer to the Congress, to the law of the land and to the citizens who voted him or her into office.

- Plan a Career Day in order to demonstrate the connection between school courses and the world of work. As a class project, make a list of community working people who can be invited to school to talk about the school-to-work connection. Be sure to ask how manners and social skills factor into their vocations and professions.

- When the class knows the vocations and professions of the guests who will be speaking on Career Day, discuss the kinds of questions you will be asking. Write these questions down so that the visit will be worthwhile for everyone. Remember, once a question has been asked, do not ask the same question again. Listen carefully.

- Follow up Career Day by writing thank-you notes to the guests who volunteered their time and interest to make the day a success!

From School to Work

A project developed by the class of Ms. Beth Pope-Kokotovich, Department of Special Education, Fitzgerald High School, Warren, Michigan.

The class was organized in partnerships to answer the question, "Why do people work?" These are their original, thoughtful responses which were dutifully recorded on a large paper pad, in multicolored markers, by the teacher.

Why Do People Work?

1. To help people
2. For money
3. For a house and car
4. For food
5. For paying bills
6. To get clothes
7. For enjoyment
8. To save money for college
9. To take care of family
10. To be successful

Why do *you* think people work?

Name _____

You may ask an adult at home or any interested grown-up of your choice.

Question

What skills did you learn in school that made it possible for you to do your job?
When you were little, what did you want to be when you grew up?

_____

_____

_____

_____

_____

_____

_____

_____

_____

_____

_____

_____

The person I interviewed was a _____

(parent, relative, neighbor, family friend, teacher)

Signature _____

WANTED

Parents interested in presenting their careers to intermediate and upper level students

Annual Career Day

_____

date

Complete the form below and return to the office.

I am interested in participating in Career Day.

Name: _____

Career: _____

Daytime Phone: _____

With permission of Dr. Ro Schilke, principal, Ferndale, Michigan Public Schools.

Dear Career Day Participant,

Thank you for your willingness to participate in Harding's fifth annual Career Day on Friday, May 23rd. Activities will begin with a reception and orientation for participants between 8:15 and 8:45 a.m. in the Teacher's Workroom. All fourth, fifth and sixth graders will have preselected their choices, and groups will consist of approximately five to eight students. There may also be some parents present.

Session times are:

Session I	8:45-9:15
Session II	9:20-9:50
Session III	9:55-10:25

Large Group Discussion   10:30-11:00 (Presenters and all students in 4-5-6 grades)

The Career Day committee understands this activity will take you away from your responsibilities and does not wish to keep you any longer than necessary. We would enjoy having you stay for the entire morning, but if that is impossible, please indicate in the appropriate place which session is most convenient for you.

The purpose of your visit will be to expand the students' understanding and appreciation of the particular career area which you represent. It is hoped that by exposing students to a variety of careers at an early age, they may become better focused on the importance of their education.

As a guideline, you may want to include in your presentation information pertaining to the following issues:

1. What are the duties of your occupation or profession?
2. What are the working hours?
3. Must special clothing be worn on the job?
4. What equipment or instruments are used? (Please bring any of the tools or instruments used in your career which will help make your career come alive for the students. If you need special equipment set up earlier, please let us know.)
5. What are the working conditions? (indoors, outdoors, noise, odors, temperature, etc.)
6. What worker characteristics are important on the job?
7. How are the subjects taught in school useful to your work?
8. Which subjects have been the most helpful?

With permission of Dr. Ro Schilke, principal, Ferndale, Michigan Public Schools.

9. In what ways do you depend on other people to help you do your work?

10. In what ways do other people depend on the work you do?

11. How does society benefit from your work?

12. Has your career area changed over the past five or 10 years?

13. What changes may happen in the future?

14. What do you like or not like about your career? (advantages/disadvantages)

15. Why and how did you select (or grow into) this occupation? (your career path . . . share ups and downs, decisions on the way)

We would welcome any visual aids, brochures, pamphlets, etc., which might illustrate or clarify major points. Also feel free to involve students in a task or assist in a demonstration.

The students are looking forward to your visit. If you have any questions, please give us a call.

Sincerely,

Ro Schilke, Principal
Mr. Dave Carlson
Ms. Wendy Mintz
Mrs. Susan Pauls
Mrs. Pat Pillott

- -

Please return as soon as possible to Harding Elementary.

I am looking forward to participating in Harding's Career Day and am available for:
_____ All three sessions   _____ Two sessions   _____One session   (Check.)

I will need the following visual aids to assist in my presentation: _____

_____

I (will, will not) be able to remain for the large group discussion.

(name) _____   (career) _____

(address) _____   (phone) _____

With permission of Dr. Ro Schilke, principal, Ferndale, Michigan Public Schools.

Pleased to Meet You

Whether you meet other people or you yourself make the introductions, this is an **important time** to **make others feel comfortable.**

That's what introductions are all about.

There are some easy guidelines to *observe* when we introduce folks. **Do your best**, and it may help you to know

that there are many adults who do not manage the task of introductions smoothly.

Some **rules** of the game and a **SENSE OF HUMOR**

will help you get through alive. Force yourself to *practice,* and you will get *better all the time.*

Meet Mr. No-Name

"I want you to meet . . ."

My mind goes blank
We stand and shuffle
I think he's Hank.

I choke right up
I feel such shame
I can't remember
What's his name.

I cough and mumble
My face gets red
Is this the guy
Whose name is Ted?

He doesn't help
I'm badly shaken
What if I'm wrong
And badly mistaken?

It's a gosh awful name
I get more tense
I know it's whacky
It makes no sense.

He smiles and extends his hand
"My name is Peter Paddywhack"
They shake and then he turns to me
"It's been a while hasn't it, Jack?"

"Hey, my name is Alphonse!"

G.B. Lipson

Pleased to Meet You

- **Keep in Mind:** Older people come first in introductions. You show respect by saying, "Grandpa, I'd like you to meet Chuckie Chover." Then say, "Chuckie, this is my grandfather, Mr. Heathcliff."

- **Keep in Mind:** Identify the people you are introducing. You say, "Mrs. Calibash, this is my dad's friend from out of town, Mr. Bob Brash." Then you repeat Bob's name. "Mr. Brash, this is my piano teacher, Mrs. Calibash."

- **Keep in Mind:** When you introduce an important person, you say that person's name first. "Colonel Crispy, I'd like you to meet my dad, Richard Strongarm." Then say, "Dad, meet Colonel Crispy."

- **Keep in Mind:** When an adult you know very well is introduced to a younger person, it is best to use Mr., Mrs., Dr. or Ms. even though you call the adult by a first name.

- **Keep in Mind:** Some husbands and wives have different last names. In that case you say, "This is Oscar Wiener and his wife Daisy Turner," or "This is Daisy Turner and her husband Oscar Wiener." The terms *partner* or *companion* are also used.

- Sometimes you are in a situation where you have not been introduced! It takes some courage, but you must take the initiative to walk up to a person, extend your hand and say, "Hi, I don't think we've met. My name is Jack Sprat."

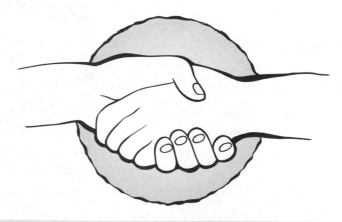

Pleased to Meet You

- **Attention, Adults, Too!** Shake hands when you are introduced. Make it firm! Do not shake as if your hand is a dead fish! This is an important lesson for a lifetime! A vigorous, brief handshake makes a good impression. Shake with energy but don't overdo it. You are not in a wrestling match.

- **Odds & Ends:** You may ask someone to repeat his or her name if you didn't quite catch it. If you are introducing your friend Debby to a girl whose name you have forgotten, try this: "I'd like you to meet my friend, Debby . . . ," then (if you are lucky) the other girl will say, "Howdy, my name is Wilma Pyle." If that doesn't happen, you may have to say to Wilma, "I'm awfully sorry, but I've forgotten your name."

Act Out

TV Introductions

Host Speaks:

"Good morning, ladies and gentlemen. I am your host, Maddy (or Manny) Manners! We have on our stage today many people who don't know one another. According to the rules above we will make different introductions in all kinds of situations. We will ask for volunteers, who will make up their own names and ages. As a guide, use all of the situations discussed above or any of your own invention."

Props:

Print signs to pin on the front of the characters to identify them for the audience. The actors may wear hats, ties or any other outfits appropriate to the situation.

Name _____

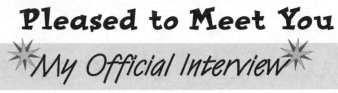
You may ask an adult at home or any interested grown-up of your choice.

Question

What was the most embarrassing introduction you have experienced or heard about?

_____

_____

_____

_____

_____

_____

_____

_____

_____

_____

_____

The person I interviewed was a _____

(parent, relative, family friend, teacher)

Signature _____

Public Behavior

Sometimes in public places, such as stores, movies, restaurants, parks, buses or malls, you may feel that there is an adult attitude you find annoying. There seems to be a prejudice that all kids are a big nuisance and have to be endured or eyed with suspicion. This is probably because adults in public places have, indeed, had bad experiences with kids who have been deliberately disruptive or plain obnoxious. It is unfair for *all* young people to be blamed for the offensive behavior of *some* kids. But it is true that there are a few kids who feel compelled to take over and bring disagreeable attention to themselves.

YOU,

personally, can be a *well-behaved* and *responsible person* who *sets a good example*.

Dear Counselor,

I'm writing this letter to you because I don't want to go to your office like a tattletale. But I need advice. I have this good friend (I'll call him Patrick) who is an all right guy when we're just hanging out. But when we go out to the mall or a movie or to Burger Butch, he acts like a clown.

It embarrasses me, and I don't know how to tell him. When we're at the movies he puts his feet up on the back of the seat in front of him like he owns the theater. Then he talks all the way through the movie. Once, somebody even called the manager!

When we go to the mall he takes his boom box and turns it up like he wants to split everybody's eardrums. People turn around and give us dirty looks.

Sometimes, when we go biking or skateboarding, he's got to show off and he doesn't seem to care even if he almost knocks people over! He acts like he owns the world and nobody else matters. What can I say to him? I think he's really a good guy, but he doesn't seem to know that other people have rights, too. How can I help Patrick so that he doesn't act like such a clown?

Sincerely,

Upset at Taft Middle School

Public Behavior

- We have all known people like Patrick. What if you were Patrick's friend? How would you describe a person like him? Why do you think Patrick acts the way he does in public?

- If you were the school counselor, what advice would you give the student who wrote the letter and signed himself "Upset at Taft Middle School." Respond by writing a letter back to him.

- In many store windows there are signs posted that say something like, "No shoes, no shirt, no service!" What does that mean and why should a store owner put up such a sign?

- Pretend that you own a sign company. The mayor comes to you and asks if you can print some colorful signs to post in public places as reminders of polite behavior. Your town of Long Branch is a lively metropolis, and the mayor's request will keep you busy for quite a while. You must make attractive signs for at least five of the following places. (Award a teacher prize for the most clever sign!) The wording is your choice.

supermarket	bowling alley
mall	filling station
museum	restaurant
sports arena	refreshment stand
doctor's/dentist's office	concert hall, theater
park	church
public property	public transportation
rest room	movie theater
public pool	elevator

- Nobody likes to be blamed for the bad behavior of a few characters. In a conversation about this subject, you hear a friend say: "Don't paint us all with the same brush!" What did she mean? (Clue: Don't make it sound like *all* teens are bad actors in public when it is only a few!)

Name _____

Public Behavior

My Official Interview

You may ask an adult at home or any interested grown-up of your choice.

Question

Describe a scene in a public place, involving teens, that you thought was *good*.

_____

_____

_____

_____

_____

_____

_____

_____

Name one kind of teen behavior you consider inappropriate in a public place.

_____

_____

The person I interviewed was a _____

(parent, relative, neighbor, family friend, teacher)

Signature _____

Let's Talk

There are times at school or in social situations when you find yourself in a place with people you don't know very well or perhaps, not at all. It is rude to stand around saying nothing! We want to be *friendly*, and so we try to **engage in conversation** as a way of creating a *comfortable situation*.

We must **practice** the **ART OF CONVERSATION** under different circumstances in order to become skilled. And, indeed, it is an art!

It is not easy to do and unfortunately some people never learn how. But *keep trying* and you will be prized as an **interesting** and **lively** guest instead of a bump on a log. Another good reason to be involved in conversation is that you may find a *new friend* who is interested in the same things that fascinate you—and that's

worth the effort!

Oh the Pain!

Alfie Blain was invited to Sammy Watnick's house where he thought there would be only the two of them, and they could horse around on the basketball court like always. At the last minute somebody told Alfie it was a birthday celebration for Sammy's sister, and he'd better get dressed up. Alfie hated the thought, but he didn't want to disappoint his friend.

He dressed up a little, but he couldn't find his good sweater. Then he realized that his best shirt was too small for him, and it was strangling him under his arms. Alfie was miserable when he walked into Sammy's house and discovered lots of people standing around. Everybody seemed to know everybody else, but he didn't even see other kids from school.

Somebody handed Alfie a dumb hat to put on his head, and he knew he'd feel like a doofus if he put it on. This was really kid stuff, he thought. Was Sammy's sister two years old? Turns out the sister's name was Molly, and she was lots older than Sammy. They sang "Happy Birthday" to her—she blew out the candles, and then they cut the cake and served ice cream. Somebody shoved a plateful at Alfie, and he started to eat.

Just then some big guy standing at Alfie's elbow said, "Do you and Sammy go to the same school?"

Alfie said, "Yes," and kept looking down and eating.

The big guy said, "Do you live down the street?"

Alfie said, "Yes," and kept eating.

Then the big guy said, "Are you and Sammy on the basketball team?"

Alfie said, "No," and as he kept eating he wished he could choke and lose consciousness and fall down on the floor and they'd have to call an ambulance and then he could get out of this so-called party.

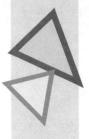

Let's Talk

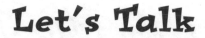

- Can you think of a solution to Alfie's uncomfortable experience? What do you think he could have done to make this situation more comfortable for himself?

- Before going further down the road, there is a very important secret to opening up a conversation which we all need to know and practice! This life-saving technique is known (in our family) as "the old-time interview technique." People are always willing to talk about themselves if you give them a chance! Besides it is flattering to have someone show an interest in you personally. This means you ask this person questions about himself or herself. **Caution:** Do not ask questions which only need "yes" or "no" answers. Those lead nowhere at all.

- **Contest! Contest!** When you are considering social conversation, **think anecdotes!** An anecdote is a short account of an interesting or humorous incident! Find a short anecdote to tell the class. Practice at home until you can deliver it to your satisfaction. It may be about a member of your family or something you read, saw or experienced. The teacher will decide on a prize for the best-told anecdote and the runner-up. (See below.)

- Why do you think people often open a conversation by talking about the weather? (It is an icebreaker and the weather is always with us.) It may not be brilliant, but at least it is one way of being conversational and hopefully *will lead into another subject.* For example: "That reminds me of my little cousin Alex who came all the way from California at Christmastime. He saw snow for the first time in his life, and when just a few flakes had fallen, he wanted his dad to go out with him and build a snow fort!"

Let's Talk

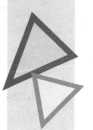

- What do you do or say when you meet someone for the first time? Be honest! Do you have any techniques which you use that work for you?

- As a class, brainstorm some topics that you would introduce if you were trying to stimulate conversation in a group of strange kids your own age. Example: "Hey, did anybody see *Slime Dweebs from Okefenokee Swamp*?"

- **Warm-Up Game:** The teacher will cut pieces of yarn in different lengths, from 12" to 16" (30 to 41 cm) long before the game starts. Pass these out to everyone in the group. One person at a time is chosen to introduce himself or herself while winding the piece of yarn around a finger. The introductory conversation must continue until the end of the yarn is reached. Then it is the next person's turn. The students must first think about how they will introduce themselves and include one interesting fact about themselves to share with the group. (The teacher must model this so that it is done slowly and is not over in five seconds.)

Act Out

In a group write out a partial script that will force some of the following characters to carry on a social conversation. Give them any kind of job, vocation or profession that will serve as material for conversation. Let your actors stretch for topics to discuss. For example:

> Your neighbors are having a get-together in the school gym. There will be music and good food, and you have been appointed as the social director. It is your job to get people warmed up, more sociable and talking together. In making your introductions it is also your responsibility to give some personal clues about the guests you bring together, hoping it will stimulate conversation. For example:

> "Abby Tuttle, I'd like you to meet my friend, Elmer Bushkey who washes elephants in the circus."

> "Abby is an auto mechanic at Duffy's Stately Garage . . ."

The participants must start talking!

Name _____

Let's Talk

My Official Interview

You may ask an adult at home or any interested grown-up of your choice.

Question

What was the most uncomfortable conversation you ever had? or What was the most wonderful conversation you ever had?

_____

_____

_____

_____

_____

_____

_____

_____

_____

_____

_____

The person I interviewed was a _____

(parent, relative, neighbor, family friend, teacher)

Signature _____

TLC10186 Copyright © Teaching & Learning Company, Carthage, IL 62321-0010

Please and Thank You, Etc.

One of the first things little children learn from parents is to say, "*Please*" and "**Thank You**." These terms are described by many people as "*the magic words*" and indeed they apply to people of all ages and all walks of life.

Our days are filled with situations where it is appropriate to use these words. They show **consideration for others**. They are *gentle gestures* and are **ALWAYS APPRECIATED** between friends and strangers alike. Hold open a door, be given something, ask for something and do something, however small, for another person, and it is a great sign of your *politeness* and **courtesy**. Think of "Excuse me," "I beg your pardon," and "Please" and "Thank you" as *gracious niceties* as well.

Magic Words

What are magic words?

Please asks for something kindly.

Please asks courteously and never demands.

Thank you shows appreciation.

Thanks shows gratitude for small and large favors.

Excuse me means "I beg your pardon."

Excuse me means "can you give me a moment?"

You're welcome means "I received your thanks."

You're welcome means "I'm glad to do it for you."

I'm sorry means "please forgive me."

I'm sorry means "I feel for your sadness."

Those are magic words!

G.B. Lipson

Please and Thank You, Etc.

- Come now. We don't really believe in magic! Magic means using sleight of hand, illusion, making things appear and disappear, charms and spells and all kinds of trick stuff. What do we mean when we speak of the "magic words" of good manners? (We are talking about words that make people feel good about one another, words that open doors, words that help us go through our days smoothly and words that help us work well with people we come in contact with every day. Those are the ways in which words do really great things for us.) Can you suggest other words or phrases that you think are special?

- There are times when we are not able to say "thank you" in person. If someone sends you a gift or remembers your birthday or another special occasion, you must send a thank-you note. First, it lets the giver know that you received it. Second, it shows your appreciation. But what do you do if you get a gift that you hate? What do you do then? (You still must realize that the person who gave it to you was thinking of you and trying to do something special for you and that is worth a sincere thank-you!)

- The classic book entitled *What Do You Say Dear?* by Sesyle Joslin was illustrated by the famous children's author, Maurice Sendak. In it he draws memorable characters in situations that call for polite responses. (Republished by Harper Row, 1986.) Try to locate this book in your school or public library. It may inspire you to produce a similar collection of hilarious situations which you, too, can illustrate.

Please and Thank You, Etc.

Student Page

The following is a shorthand method of illustrating polite phrases:

I'll have a hot fudge sundae with lots of whipped cream and a cherry, please!

You're welcome, kids!

Thanks for supper, Mom!

I'm sorry your turtle died.

Excuse me for stepping on your toes.

I'm sorry your grandpa is sick.

Expanding Polite Phrases!

When
When you
When you say
When you say let
When you say let me
When you say let me lend
When you say let me lend you
When you say let me lend you a
When you say let me lend you a helping
When you say let me lend you a helping hand
When you say let me lend you a helping hand, friend.
    It will make you feel 10 feet tall!

Let's
Let's talk
Let's talk about
Let's talk about magic
Let's talk about magic words
Let's talk about magic words that
Let's talk about magic words that make
Let's talk about magic words that make good
Let's talk about magic words that make good things
Let's talk about magic words that make good things happen!

Now you try it in any artistic arrangement you like.

        G.B. Lipson

Name _____

Pretend that you received a really wonderful gift (your choice). Write a warm and sincere thank-you note to the person who sent it to you. Describe the reasons why you loved the gift. Make them feel pleased that they took the time and trouble just for you.

_____

_____

_____

_____

_____

_____

_____

_____

_____

_____

_____

_____

_____

96

Help Others

Learning to help others radiates into many areas of your daily activity. It is important at home, school, community and in far-reaching areas.

Becoming a **helping person** is a way of building your life upon a very special ideal.

It means **caring about people** you may not even know; it means that you **give** a portion of your **STRENGTH** and *energy* to aid others; it means that you **serve** those who need your **support** in small and large ways.

Young and old alike are able to give a **HELPING HAND** in many situations—it only requires *willingness* and an **awareness** that your efforts are needed.

Since *kindness* is not limited by age, we all need to make room in our lives for *greater care* for **those who are needy**.

Smash Up!

It was bitter cold and blowing when Cindy walked out of the house to get into her old car. What a break that her sister had loaned her this big oversized winter coat! These daybreak trips to work were tough, but the job was good and the people were so friendly every morning.

Cindy worked in a little restaurant called the Athenium Beanery. Everybody joked about the name of the place, but it was very popular because they had the best food in town. The cook, Mr. Matto, was a soup genius and customers, plain and fancy, rich and poor, came just for a bowl of his bean soup!

Luckily Cindy had flexible hours. It was good that way because she could get to classes at Oakland Community College, have time for homework and still earn enough toward her tuition payments. Pleasant thoughts about work and school drifted in and out of her mind as she entered the ramp onto Interstate 696.

Winter winds swayed her poor car, but Cindy was grateful she had wheels in this weather. The car trembled as if it were just managing to stay on course. A morning radio broadcast was announcing more harsh weather and falling temperatures. Cindy hated it when they did that little arithmetic thing with the windchill factor which made it feel even worse.

The snow was falling in big, sticky globs. It was blinding and started to whip across the freeway. Cindy slowed down. Time for more caution now, she said to herself. Heads up! Just then she checked her rearview mirror. To her horror she saw a sporty red car coming at full tilt—as if the road was a race-track. Like a hydroplane it skimmed the surface pavement at high speed passing her in a flash.

For a moment she was relieved until she saw a frightening picture unfold ahead. The red car cut sharply in front of a truck as the transport driver braked heavily to avoid it. The slick pavement played its ghastly mischief—the truck skidded—came full around, careening out of control. Straight as a missile it sped toward Cindy's car head-on! The red car disappeared into nowhere when the collision with Cindy and the truck echoed under the overpass of the freeway.

A few people slowed down. There were the usual gawkers and other curious people who took a brief look in passing. Then a gray-haired man pulled over onto the shoulder of the road and rushed out toward the smashed car. He forced the car door open and started to talk softly to Cindy, "Don't move—everything will be all right," he reassured her. "The police are on their way right this minute." He stroked her hair gently out of her eyes.

There was a strange wetness on her face and she thought her mouth was bleeding. He quieted her rising panic in a soft voice. "It's okay; you'll be just fine," he kept repeating and reassuring her. She felt her cold hand in his warm one. He never left her side, and though she wished for her mother, he was a kind and concerned presence. He hovered as the emergency medical people strapped her to a board and secured her in the ambulance.

Other sounds floated in through a mist of confusion.
"She must have hit the steering wheel."
"Yeah, but the seat belt saved her from going through the windshield."
"Lucky if all she has are black eyes."
"She's in pain when she breathes."
"Must be broken ribs."
"That heavy overcoat was a help . . ."

The rest was a blur. The last voice she remembered was his—"I'll hold good thoughts for you," he said.

She didn't know his name, but she would never forget him. To her sorrow she had not thanked him for his tenderness to a strange girl in a wrecked car on Interstate 696.

G.B. Lipson

Help Others

- Cindy said she would never forget the old man. He wasn't a doctor–how then did he come to her rescue? What did he do that made him so important to her?

- *USA Weekend* is a publication which is a Sunday insert supplement which appears in 496 major newspapers. Since 1990 it has sponsored the "Make a Difference Day" on October 25th of every year. People of all ages are encouraged to do something for others on that day through schools, religious affiliations, Girl and Boy Scouts, 4-H Clubs, hospitals, homeless shelters, business and social agencies. Ordinary people and celebrities participate in activities which include projects such as performing, cleaning, painting, tutoring, helping with environmental tasks, planting and all manners of volunteering. The projection is that in 1997 one million Americans will volunteer and support this effort. For more information for your school community, check your local newspapers and libraries.

- There is nothing quite as gratifying as working shoulder to shoulder with all kinds of people who are doing good works! If your class were to develop a project to help your community or school, what would it be? Make suggestions that may be listed on the board. Break into groups to decide on your class effort. How would you go about lending your collective hands?

- Make a chart that recognizes helpers in your class. Entitle it *Helping Hands*. List the name of a person who was an outstanding helper of the week. Create your own class helpers' logo. Consider making T-shirts with that same logo and a catchy phrase.

The Detroit News and Free Press, October 17-19, 1997, *USA Weekend*, pp. 4-7.

Name _____

Help Others

Student Page

No matter how big or how small, what was the very best thing you ever did to help someone? How did it make you feel?

_____

_____

_____

_____

_____

_____

_____

_____

_____

_____

_____

_____

_____

_____

102

Gossip and Rumors

GOSSIP IS LIKE POISON

because it spreads,

it is harmful and it causes injury!

Rumors start with one person who tells another

and another until pretty soon the story has a life

of its own. The details or the facts get blurred

and changed from mouth to mouth until it

no longer resembles the truth.

Gossip and rumors are hard to trace—

Who started it?

How did it begin?

Can it be believed?

Is there a grain of truth in any of it?

Gossip of a personal nature can hurt

individuals or groups of people and the

victims are powerless to do anything about it.

Wildfire

There were some changes in the Sanilac school schedule that day because the painters had come in to paint the walls in the East Corridor. The sign on the door of the English classroom 322 directed the kids to Mr. Carter's shop room.

Phew! Some of the kids hated the smell of linseed oil in the shop class. They filed in—grumbling all the while. Some tried to find seats that would be close to the chalkboard, while they avoided a lot of junk on the floor.

Just then, Megan, a hall monitor, came in and announced to the kids that there was another change. "Too many complaints from the smell in this room," she said. "You're s'posed to go back to room 322! I'll lock this door."

The kids filed out quickly, happy to leave. As Megan was walking to the door she saw a pile of rags smoldering on a shop table. She was sure that smoke was coming from it. Was that a flicker or a flame? Her heart dropped.

Without thinking of her personal safety, Megan swooped up the rags and walked slowly, deliberately toward the sink. She didn't want to fan this dangerous armful as she felt the heat against her arms. She plopped the stuff into the deep sink and turned on the water full force! Megan had truly saved the day.

Proud of her fast thinking, she went to the principal's office to report the incident. And then the rumors started to fly. Somebody said there was a serious fire in the room and some kids got trampled leaving the room.

Another story was that the corridor filled with smoke just as the fire trucks arrived. Someone described the furniture being chopped to bits by the fire fighters—some of whom staggered out with smoke inhalation. The rumors spread to the parents at lunchtime, and they descended on the school in a panic. A few people thought that a teacher would be dismissed because of the incident. Or was the fire set on purpose?

G.B. Lipson

Gossip and Rumors

- How did you think this story about the fire in the shop class got started and spread all over the community? What could one person have said that created such an overblown incident?

- There is a game called Rumor that starts with a carefully selected sentence. The first person reads the sentence and whispers it into the ear of a classmate. The message is then repeated over and over again from ear to ear. **You are not allowed to repeat the message** if somebody says, "Hey, I didn't hear that properly!" When the last person receives the final message, it is to be announced to the entire class. Was it accurate? Was it twisted? How did it compare to the original message?

- Very often gossip is a tale which is personal about someone. Often it is mean and very hurtful. How would you feel it someone were telling a nasty story that made you and other people laugh and then you discovered the story was about you?

- Mothers and fathers often have words of wisdom that are so sensible that the saying stays with you forever. My mother always said, "Anyone who gossips to you will gossip about you." Think about that. What does it mean? Do you agree or disagree? Why?

- Invent some mottoes to discourage gossip and unkind words. Draw a strong, dramatic picture to go along with the motto that will catch attention. Make them clever and catchy.

  1. Spread peanut butter not rumors.

  2. Don't carry tales (tails).

  3. Don't believe everything you hear.

- Now it's your turn.

Gossip and Rumors

Act Out

Here is an exercise that illustrates how information can be twisted as it is processed.

Select a story with a number of details.

Ask for three volunteers (Teller 1, Teller 2, Teller 3).

Send two Tellers out of the room.

Keep Teller 1 in the room to listen to the story with the class.

After the teller hears the story, he or she will go out of the room and tell the story **only to Teller 2**. No one else must hear!

Teller 2 comes into the room and tells the class what he thinks he heard.

Teller 2 goes out of the room and tells Teller 3 who then comes back into the room and recounts the story for the last time!

Select a story with a number of details. You may enhance it however you choose, but don't make it too long because the audience will be hearing the story several times. If things work right, the changes in the story will be lots of fun and demonstrate how information from one person to another gets distorted! But! If it does or does not remain accurate to the original, everyone will have earned a round of applause!

Gossip and Rumors

The following abridged selection is a good example. Expand on it as you wish.

1. A little bird is dying of the cold at the side of a country road, during a horrible winter.

2. A farmer comes along, and he wants to save the bird. He wraps it in a rag from his wagon and departs. But the bird is still dying of the cold.

3. Another farmer comes along and sees the bird wrapped in the rag. He thinks mud will make the bird warmer, and so he mixes snow and dirt together.

4. He wraps the bird in the mud and departs. The bird feels warmer and warmer. He is so grateful that he starts to sing with joy.

5. A third farmer comes along and hears the bird singing. He picks up the bird and sees him in the coat of mud. He misunderstands and thinks the bird wants to be released from the mud. He cleans the mud off the little creature like a good Samaritan. He leaves and, as you would expect, the poor bird gets cold again and freezes to death.

6. The moral of the story is, "When you're covered with mud up to your neck, you had better not sing."

Name _____

Gossip and Rumors

Student Page

What is the silliest gossip you ever heard or read?

_____

_____

_____

_____

_____

_____

_____

_____

_____

_____

_____

_____

_____

_____

_____

_____

Dear Teacher,

Depending upon your group of children and the level of interest of parents, you may want to invite the folks at home to participate in the skills and manners unit of study.

Do they have suggestions for additional topics they would like to see developed? Using the organization of the book as a template (starting with the concept, then with activities and finally with the students' opinions), are there general suggestions derived from specific instances they would like to see addressed?

As the writing of this book progressed, I consulted more teachers and parents for their views. Some of their interesting suggestions were straightforward, some were commonly mentioned and a few were somewhat embarrassing and/or off-limits.

There were those who wanted more adult interviews in tandem with the opinions of the students. To this end, two extra pages are included—one is an adult interview page and the other is a student page. Each of these pages allows for the subject of your choice.

Do feel free to accommodate whatever innovations are suggested by the students and their parents thereby enriching the tie between the home and school. Adapt what you will to the sentiments and disposition of your group, and consider the book just a beginning to an enduring effort that takes years to refine.

Name _____

You may ask an adult at home or any interested grown-up of your choice.

Question

_____

_____

_____

_____

_____

_____

_____

_____

_____

_____

_____

_____

The person I interviewed was a _____

(parent, relative, neighbor, family friend, teacher)

Signature _____

Name _____

Topic

_____

_____

_____

_____

_____

_____

_____

_____

_____

_____

_____

_____

_____

_____

_____

Recognition Certificate

Awarded to

_____

For demonstration of good manners and social skills!

Presented by

_____

_____
date